NORTHUMBERLAND SLS	
3201778127	
Bertrams	10/11/2008
S745.5	£12.99

Make Your Own Art

Paper Folding

FRANKLIN WATTS

LONDON • SYDNEY

First published in 2008 by Franklin Watts

© 2008 Arcturus Publishing Limited

Franklin Watts
338 Euston Road
London NW1 3BH

Franklin Watts Australia
Level 17/207 Kent Street, Sydney, NSW 2000

Produced by Arcturus Publishing Limited,
26/27 Bickels Yard, 151–153 Bermondsey Street,
London SE1 3HA

Editor: Alex Woolf
Designers: Sally Henry and Trevor Cook
Consultant: Daisy Fearns

Picture credits: Sally Henry and Trevor Cook

Every attempt has been made to clear copyright.
Should there be any inadvertent omission,
please apply to the publisher for rectification.

A CIP catalogue record for this book is available
from the British Library.

Dewey Decimal Classification Number: 736'.98

ISBN 978 0 7496 8192 0

Printed in China

Franklin Watts is a division of Hachette Children's Books,
an Hachette Livre UK company
www.hachettelivre.co.uk

Contents

BANG

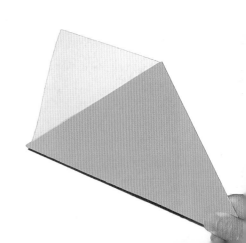

Introduction

The art of folding paper is almost as old as paper itself. Paper was invented in the east, and there are many ancient paper folding designs. Old and new designs all share the same basic requirements for success.

Paper

Use ordinary quality, coloured office copier type A4-size paper, unless the instructions say otherwise. It's fun to use all sorts of paper, though. Try patterned paper, such as wrapping paper. It's usually printed on one side and plain white on the other. Coloured art paper comes in sizes much bigger than office paper, so it's good for a special project.

To make the flowers on page 16, you can use tissue paper or crêpe paper.

Tissue paper comes in bright colours. It is thin enough to let light shine through it, making the colours bright but natural looking.

Crêpe paper is thicker than tissue and is made with lots of tiny creases. This means that by gently pulling at it, you can stretch the paper so that it's no longer flat, but curved.

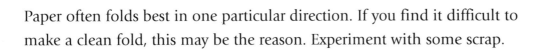

Paper often folds best in one particular direction. If you find it difficult to make a clean fold, this may be the reason. Experiment with some scrap.

Fold

The dotted line shows where the fold should be made. The arrow shows which direction to make the fold. There is usually an edge or a point that the folded part has to meet.

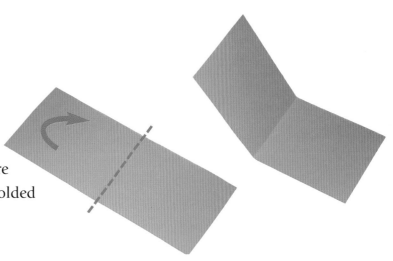

Crease

Make a fold in a sheet of paper and open it out again. The mark left is a crease. Depending on the design, you can use this as a fold later in the construction, or you might just use it as a guide to get other folds in the right place.

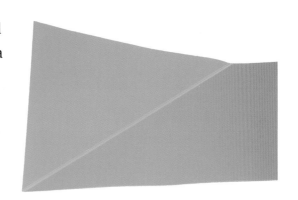

Burnished fold

When you want a fold to be really crisp and lay flat, or a crease to be very clear, use a tool to burnish the fold. Make the fold very carefully, and check it is accurate. Then gently rub down the fold using a tool such as a ruler or the back of a spoon.

Tricky folds

Take care when one end of the fold meets another fold. Try to make this a crisp angle.

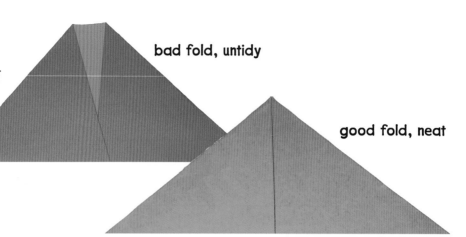

bad fold, untidy

good fold, neat

Curling paper

Sometimes you may want to make your paper bend or curl. You can make paper gently curl by wrapping it round a pencil.

Steadily pulling it under the edge of a ruler will make a tighter curl, depending on how hard you pull it.

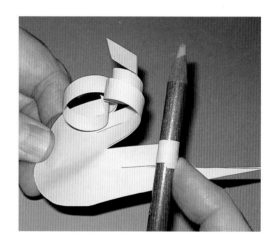

Lining paper

For really large folding projects and especially for hats lining paper is ideal. It comes on rolls and you can buy it quite cheaply at DIY stores.

Glue

You may need one of two sorts of glue. The sort that comes as a **glue stick** is ideal for sticking flat pieces of paper to paper. Place the piece to be glued face down on a clean piece of scrap paper and apply the glue evenly, working towards the edge. You can use it for putting the bits of decoration on the snappers (see page 22).

Universal glue that comes in a tube is best for sticking odd-shaped bits together, and for sticking paper to other materials. Use it for sticking the leaves to the stems of the flowers (see page 16). This glue dries clear but try to avoid getting it on the front of your work. Use a matchstick to spread this glue on small items.

Decorating paper

If you want to paint patterns or designs on your paper folding, do it before you start, not on the finished work. This is much neater, and will make the result more impressive!

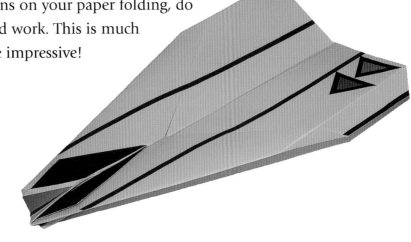

Windmills

The paper WINDMILL is a real old favourite. It's so simple to make. Enjoy creating our model with your friends.

10 MINUTES

1 MINUTE

8

You will need:

- *Thin card or coloured paper, pins, sticks*
- *Scissors, ruler or set square, pencil*

What to do...

Work on a table, measure a square
200 x 200mm (8 x 8in) on your card.

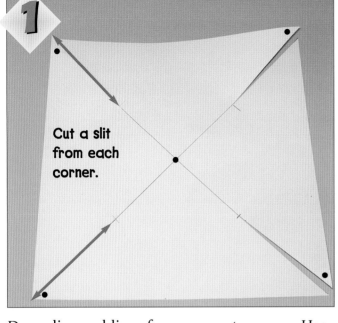

Cut a slit from each corner.

Draw diagonal lines from corner to corner. Use scissors to cut 100 mm (4in) along the lines. Make a small hole in the centre and to the side of each triangle.

Put a pin through one corner hole and bend the paper over to the middle.

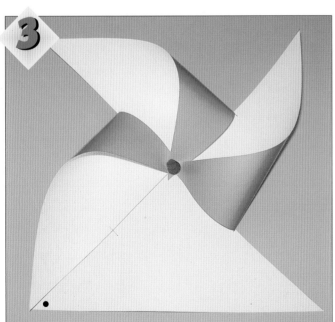

When you have gathered all four corners together, push the pin through the centre hole and press it into the top of a stick.
Adjust the pin so the windmill turns freely.

It's best to decorate your windmill before you assemble it.

Gift boxes

A cleverly folded box that you've made yourself is a novel way to present gifts of sweets or small toys. Make this design without using glue. You'll be surprised how useful it can be.

You will need:

- *Thin card or thick paper*
- *Scissors, ruler*
- *Wrapped sweets (optional)*

5
MINUTES

What to do...

Start with a piece of paper 150 x 150mm (6 x 6in). Fold the short sides together and make a light crease.

0
MINUTES

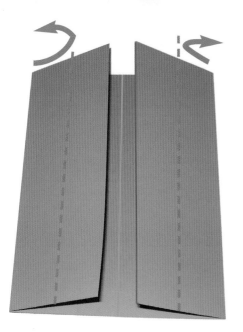

1 Open the paper out and fold the short sides in to meet the centre crease.

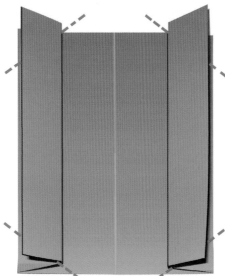

2 Fold back the flaps to the edges. Fold the four corners inwards to the creases.

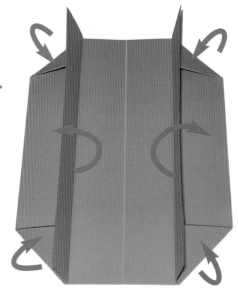

3 Fold the top flaps back and burnish them down firmly. Turn the paper over.

4 We have bent the bottom part up. Now bend the top part down at the crease, so that you see squares at the corners.

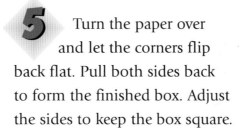

5 Turn the paper over and let the corners flip back flat. Pull both sides back to form the finished box. Adjust the sides to keep the box square.

6 Add wrapped sweets.

Use patterned paper too!

High flyers

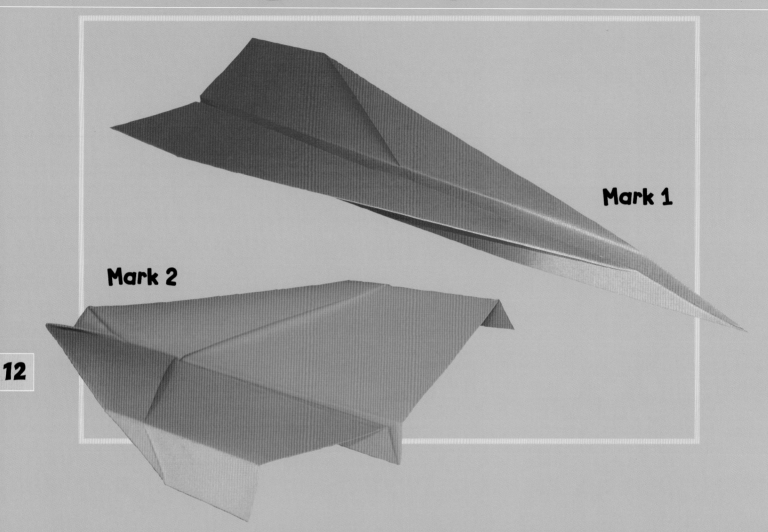

Mark 1

Mark 2

You may know how to make the Mark 1 – the paper dart, but what about the Mark 2? It has lots more folds, but is it a better flyer?

You will need:

- *Coloured paper (A4 size) or white office paper*
- *Ruler*
- *Paper clip*

10 MINUTES

What to do...

Work on a desk or table. You need to make sharp, accurate folds. Follow steps 1 to 4 for the Mark 1 glider. Go for steps 5 to 9 for the Mark 2. This one should be ace!

2 MINUTES

1

Fold the paper lengthways, crease and open flat.

2

Fold the top corners to the middle, then fold again.

3

Fold the sides into the middle. Go to step 4 for Mark 1, step 5 for Mark 2.

4

Mark 1 only

Fold the wings out 25mm (1in) from the edge.

5

Fold the tip down to touch the point where the folds meet.

6

Fold the sides into the middle.

7

Fold on the dotted lines to make winglets.

8

Fold the wings out 12mm (0.5in) from the edge.

13

9 Hold the centre of the plane. The wings should form a V shape. Add a paper clip to the nose. Adjust the winglets and the angle of the wings for best results. Experiment as much as you like for a perfect flight!

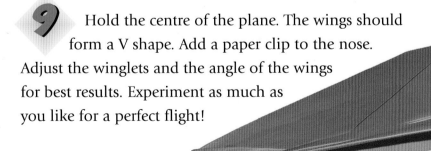

paper clip

cross section of the plane

Party hats

Party hats are essential for getting a party to go well. Follow these easy steps to make a feathered hat and a crown in no time!

You will need:

- *Coloured paper (A3)*
- *Coloured feathers, shiny stars*
- *Scissors, glue stick, stapler*
- *Marker pens, pencil*

25 MINUTES

What to do...

For our first hat, we've used paper that's blue on one side and white on the other to make the folding easier to follow. Fold the paper lengthways to make a crease, then flatten it.

5 MINUTES

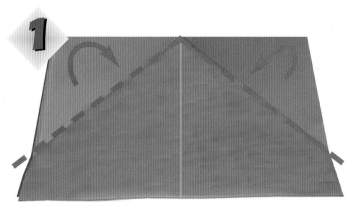

1

Fold the paper short side to short side. Fold the corners to meet the centre crease.

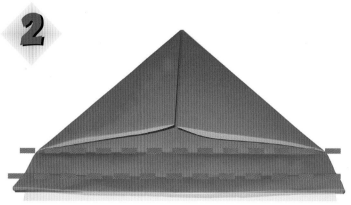

2

Take the strip below the triangle and fold the top layer in half, and then up.

3

Turn over, and fold the lower edge as in stage 2. Pull the sides outwards to form the hat.

4

Make a diamond-shaped badge from paper and a shiny star. Tape some feathers behind it. Fix the badge with glue.

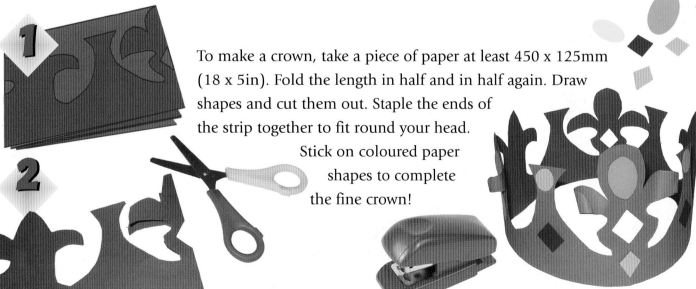

1

2

To make a crown, take a piece of paper at least 450 x 125mm (18 x 5in). Fold the length in half and in half again. Draw shapes and cut them out. Staple the ends of the strip together to fit round your head. Stick on coloured paper shapes to complete the fine crown!

Paper flowers

Make five or six of these lovely PAPER FLOWERS and they will make
a colourful bouquet for someone you like.

You will need:

- Coloured tissue paper
- Coloured crêpe paper
- Coloured pipe-cleaners
- Universal glue
- Scissors, a pencil

25 MINUTES

What to do...

We're going to make flowers
with tissue paper petals and
some coloured pipe-cleaners
for stems. You can experiment
with crêpe paper as well.

5 MINUTES

1 Fold some squares of tissue paper into quarters. Cut petal shapes out of the unfolded sides. Snip the point off the corner of the folded paper.

2 Open the tissue paper to reveal petal shapes. Cut three different sizes.

3 Fold some squares of green paper and cut into spiky leaf shapes. Snip the point off the corner to make a hole.

17

4 Put one of each size of petal shapes on top of each other. Put the spiky leaf shape at the bottom.

5 Use a pipe-cleaner for the stem. Fold black tissue into a roll and snip it to make a fringe. Wind this around the top of the stem and glue it on.

6 Push the bottom of the stem down through the holes in the petal shapes. Put glue on the green spiky leaf shape and stick it in place, underneath the petals.

Make leaves from crêpe paper. Fix them to the stem with glue.

Make the stem form a spiral by winding it around a pencil.

Zigzag frame

You can easily make a ZIGZAG FRAME to fit a picture or favourite photo. We've put our paper flowers in a frame!

You will need:

- White card
- Coloured paper
- Corrugated paper
- Universal glue
- Scissors, pencil, ruler
- Paper flowers or a picture

30 MINUTES

What to do...

Measure your picture first. Cut the white card to size – 120mm (4in) bigger both ways.

5 MINUTES

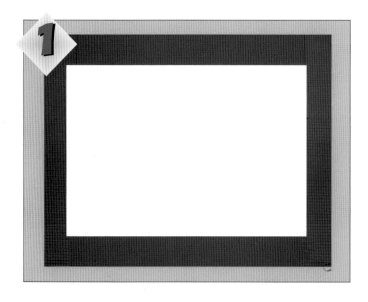

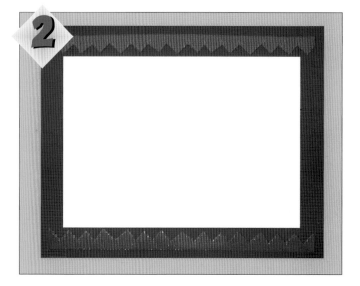

Use corrugated card or coloured paper to make four edging strips. We made ours the same width as our ruler. Glue them to the edges of your white card.

Cut another strip of paper or card in a bright colour. Make it twice as wide as the edging and as long as the frame. Mark a zigzag down the strip so that you can cut out two pieces of border pattern. Stick them top and bottom.

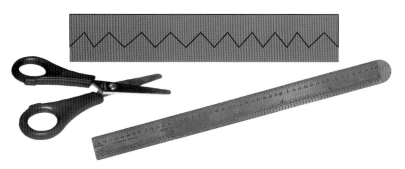

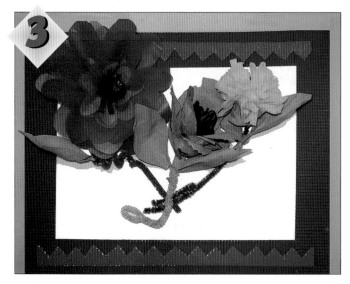

We've used paper flowers from the last project and arranged them inside the frame.

Stick them down firmly and glue on a simple bowl shape to hide the stems.

Paper banger

These BANGERS are harmless but can be very noisy! They are easily made from a cereal box and a sheet of office paper. Amaze your friends, but remember to keep bangers away from teachers!

10
MINUTES

2
MINUTES

You will need:

- *Empty cereal box*
- *Office paper (A4)*
- *Marker pen, ruler*
- *Glue stick*
- *Scissors*
- *Ear plugs (optional)*

What to do...

Our banger is made of two triangles. One is card, measuring 380 x 270 x 270mm (15 x 10.5 x 10.5in), and one is paper 270 x 190 x 190mm (10.5 x 7.5 x 7.5in) with 12mm (0.5in) flaps on the short sides. Card from a cereal packet is ideal.

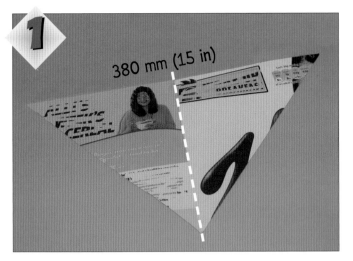

Carefully fold the card triangle in two.

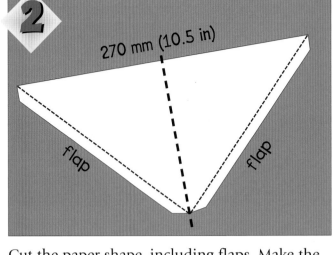

Cut the paper shape, including flaps. Make the folds as shown.

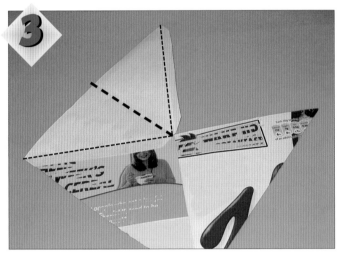

Glue one flap of the paper to the matching inner edge of the card.

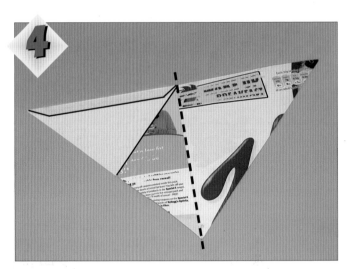

Fold the office paper in and glue the other flap. Close the card triangle down onto the flap.

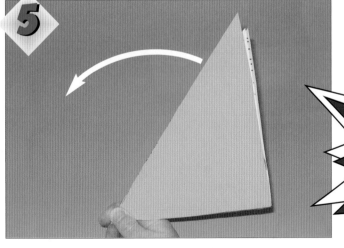

To make the banger work, hold the corner without the paper and swing!

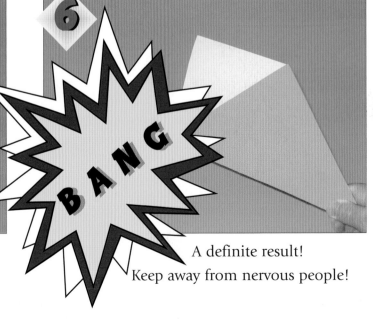

A definite result!
Keep away from nervous people!

Snappers

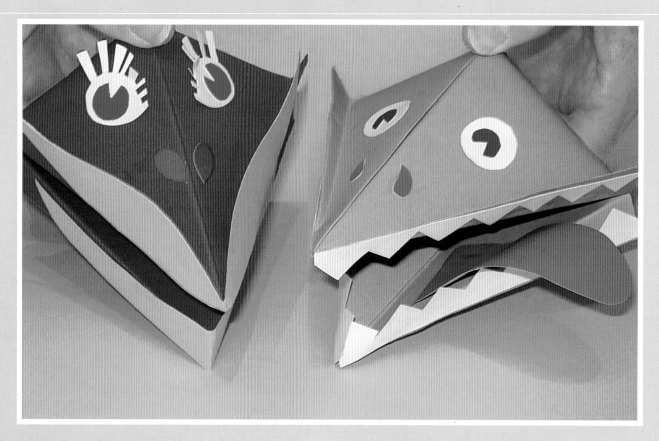

SNAPPERS are quick to make. Once you have the basic shape it's easy to customise by adding different kinds of eyes, eyelashes, nostrils, teeth and tongues. Snappers are spring-loaded and can be animated by opening and closing your hand.

15
MINUTES

2
MINUTES

You will need:

- *Coloured paper*
- *Scissors*
- *Glue stick*
- *Pencil*

What to do...

Choose some really brightly coloured paper to build snappers. Follow the steps 1 to 9. Take care to make sharp folds as you create your snapper. You could challenge your friends to see who can make the most spectacular snapper!

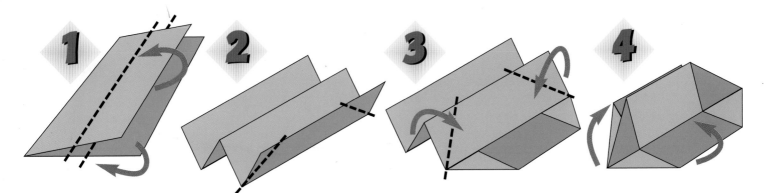

Use a square of paper about 200 x 200mm (8 x 8in). Fold it in half, open out, then fold the sides back to the middle.

Fold over the corners of the first section to meet the first fold.

Fold over the corners of the second section to meet the same fold.

Fold over the corners of the last section to meet the fold on that side. Bring the sides up.

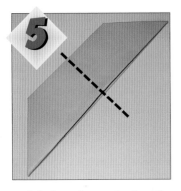

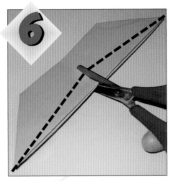

Fold the shape in half to find the centre.

Make a 12mm (0.5in) cut along the fold through both sides.

Fold the long triangles back on both sides.

Pull the sides apart.

23

Fold it over so that the points meet.

Open and close the snapper by moving your fingers and thumb. Stick on eyes, zigzag teeth, nostrils and tongue.

Give your snapper different features to make him unique.

Fortune teller

This FORTUNE TELLER will be popular, as most people are curious about their future! Write some really interesting fortunes for your friends and family.

You will need:

- *Coloured or office paper*
- *Scissors, ruler*
- *Marker pen*
- *Stick-on shapes*

10 MINUTES

What to do...

You need a square of paper about 200 x 200mm (8 x 8in). Follow stages 1 to 5 carefully and you will soon have a fun object to amuse your friends.

0 MINUTES

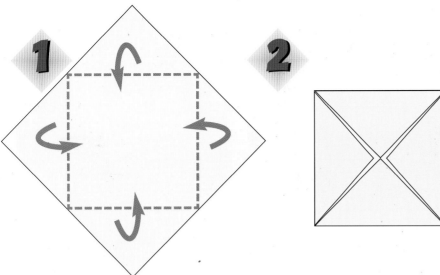

1 Fold the corners of your paper to the middle.

2 This makes a smaller square. Now turn the paper over.

3 Fold the new corners over into the middle, as before.

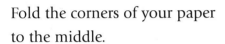
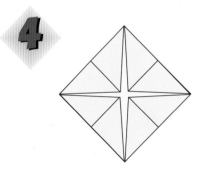

4 Keep the paper folded and turn it over. You should see four square flaps.

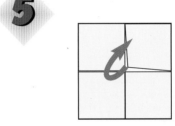

5 Lift the flaps and put your fingers and thumbs inside to bring the four points together. (See main picture opposite.)

6 Put on the coloured stickers. Write the figures 1 to 8 and the eight messages inside.

7 Ask your friend to choose a colour and a number. Open and close the fortune teller

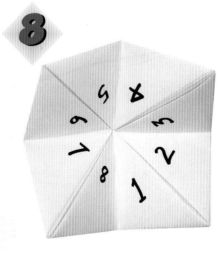

8 with your fingers and thumbs, counting out loud up to the number. Open at the chosen

9 number and read off their fortune! Good news is best!

Water bomb !

You can fill this clever paper box with water and throw it at a friend on a hot day! It will take you two minutes to make and you don't need glue!

You will need:

- *Coloured office paper*
- *Scissors, ruler*
- *Tap water*

2
MINUTES

What to do...

Cut your paper into squares. A 200 x 200mm (8 x 8in) square is a good size to start with. It will make a water bomb a bit smaller than a tennis ball.

?
MINUTES

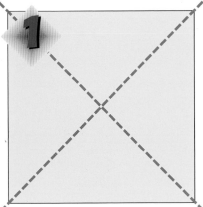

1

Fold your square of paper corner to corner both ways.

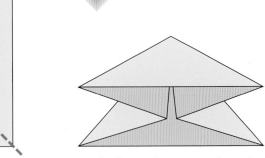

2

Push the sides in so that the paper folds on the creases, making a triangle shape.

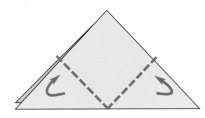

3

Fold the corners of the top layer up to the middle point.

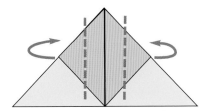

4

Fold over the corners of the flaps to meet in the middle.

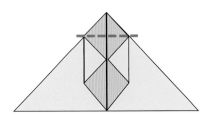

5

Fold down the top points of the triangle.

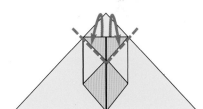

6

Fold the small triangles over and tuck into the folds left and right.

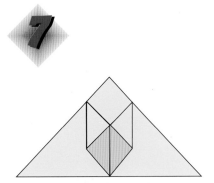

7

Turn the paper over and repeat steps 3 to 6.

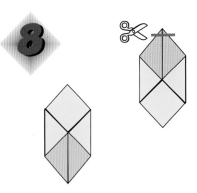

8

Turn the paper upside down and snip or tear off the tip of the point made up of folds.

9

Blow air into the bomb to inflate it. Fill the bomb with tap water and you are ready for testing!

Swan Mobile

25
MINUTES

5
MINUTES

You will need:

- White card, scissors, glue stick
- Thin barbecue stick–200mm (8in)
- Office paper, photocopies, tracing paper, a pin
- Dark thread, black and coloured marker pens

What to do...

You can trace or photocopy our templates on page 30.

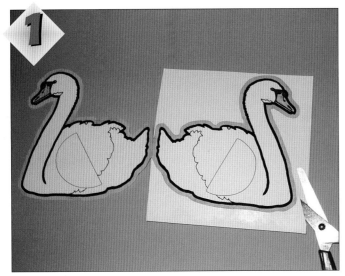

1

Stick a photocopy of the big double swan to card, or draw the large swan on both sides of white card. Work in pencil, then go round the edge in thick black marker. Cut the swans out, leaving a border, which you can colour pale blue. Colour their beaks orange.

2 Cut two wing shapes for each swan from white office paper, using the templates on page 30.

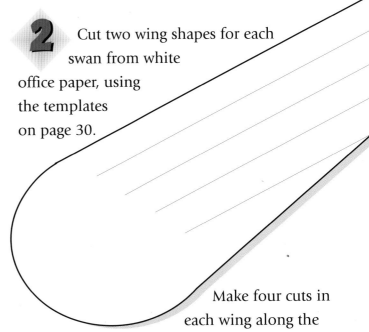

Make four cuts in each wing along the fine lines. Curl the paper by wrapping each strip around a pencil. Make sure your wings are in pairs, left and right. Stick the rounded part of the wings onto the outline patches on the swan.

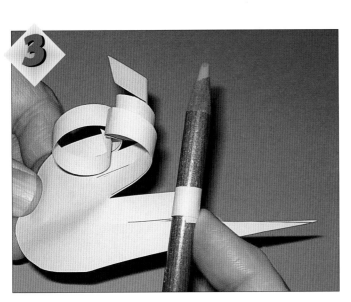

3

Repeat the process until you have one large swan and at least three smaller ones. A dot on the top of the swan's back indicates where the thread should be fixed. Allow plenty of thread for each swan. Fix the big swan using a short thread to the middle of the stick.

4

Make a hole with a pin and attach a thread. Tie each swan with a knot.

Suspend one smaller swan at each end of the stick. Put the last swan in the middle, but hanging lower. Ensure all the swans can move freely. Ask an adult to help you. Check the picture on the page opposite.

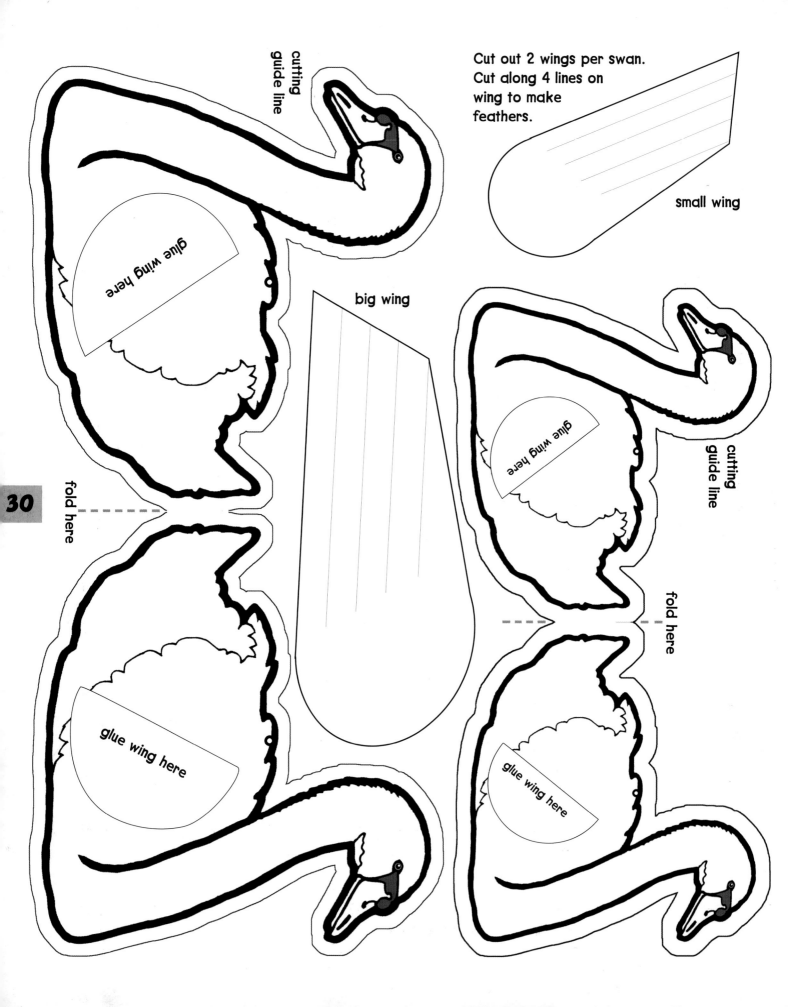

cutting
guide line

Cut out 2 wings per swan.
Cut along 4 lines on
wing to make
feathers.

small wing

glue wing here

big wing

glue wing here

fold here

cutting
guide line

30

fold here

glue wing here

glue wing here

Glossary

Cardboard
Boxes for packaging are made of cardboard. It's often dull grey or brown.

Corrugated paper
A special kind of board made from two layers of paper with a wavy layer of paper glued between them. It's a very strong sort of paper.

Crease
A crease is the mark left by folding card or paper and flattening it out again.

Crêpe paper
This is a special sort of craft paper made with lots of little wrinkles in it. You can pull it into curved shapes like flower petals.

Diagonal
A diagonal is a line that joins the corners of a square or rectangle.

Diamond-shaped
A four-sided shape, pointed top and bottom and at both sides.

Mobile
A mobile is an artwork that can move. They're often made to hang from the ceiling.

Oblong
An oblong is a shape like a square, but longer one way than the other.

Palette
This is a tray or board that you mix up paints in. It can also mean the range of colours that you are using.

Parallel
Lines the same distance apart (like railway tracks) are parallel.

Pipe-cleaner
It used to be used to clean smokers' pipes. Now there are coloured ones for craft work.

Rectangle
It's the same as an oblong.

Set square
A guide you use to make sure angles are 90°.

set square

Staple
A wire fastener you use to fix paper together.

Template
Sometimes called a pattern, a template is a guide for making lots of things the same shape. There are some on the opposite page!

Tissue paper
You can buy coloured tissue paper from craft shops. Tissue paper is very thin and is also used for protecting fragile things. Always ask if you can have wrapping paper for your work!

Tracing paper
Thin but strong paper you can see through. Put it on top of something you want to copy and draw on it.

Index